Journey through the Solar System

Simon Abbott

The Solar System

Earth is one of eight planets travelling, or orbiting, around the Sun. Together the Sun and planets make up our Solar System. Let's blast off into space and find out more...

The four planets closest to the Sun – Mercury, Venus, Earth and Mars – are rocky places.

The Sun is a star, which means it makes light and heat.

Mercury

Venus

Earth

You are here.

Mars

The Asteroid Belt is a band of millions of lumps of rock, all orbiting the Sun.

Jupiter, Saturn, Uranus and Neptune are made of gas, so there's no solid surface to walk on!

Neptune

Uranus

Saturn

Jupiter

The Solar System contains dwarf planets, moons, asteroids, comets, stardust and invisible gases, too.

Lift Off!

Since the first human shot into space in 1961, more than 500 people have followed. Some people have lived for months in space on board the **International Space Station.**

Space Travel Timeline

'One small step for a man, one giant leap for mankind.'

1969
Neil Armstrong is the first person to walk on the Moon, during the **Apollo 11** mission.

1961
Yuri Gagarin is the first human to travel into space. He circles Earth once in his spacecraft **Vostok 1.**

1957
Laika the dog becomes the first animal to orbit Earth.

The Future

When you're older, you may be able to take a trip into space with other tourists in a space plane.

2000

The first astronauts stay at the **International Space Station** and carry out experiments about life in space.

1981

The first reusable spacecraft is launched. Later shuttle missions help to build the **International Space Station (ISS)**.

The Moon

The Moon is a big ball of rock that orbits Earth. Astronauts have landed on the Moon six times between 1969 and 1972 in the Apollo missions.

The astronaut **Alan Shepard** hit a golf ball on the Moon. It travelled a huge distance and is still there today!

The surface of the Moon is made of grey, rocky soil. Astronauts collected many samples during their missions.

The Moon is covered in massive dents called craters.

Astronauts left a mirror on the Moon's surface to help with space experiments.

We see different views, or phases, of the Moon, depending on how much is lit by the Sun.

New Moon

Crescent

First Quarter

Waxing Gibbous

Full Moon

Waning Gibbous

Last Quarter

Crescent

The astronauts explored the surface in an **electric buggy**.

Some equipment was left on the Moon to collect more information.

Did You Know?
The Moon mission computers were only as powerful as a modern pocket calculator!

Zoom to the Moon!
It would take 30 days to get to the Moon by car, but it took the Apollo astronauts just 13 hours.

WOW!

The Moon is hotter than boiling water during the day, and colder than a freezer at night-time.

The Sun

Our star, the Sun, is a ginormous ball of fiery gases.
It gives us the light and warmth we need to live.

The Sun's surface bubbles with heat and energy, which travels from its hottest part at its middle.

Energy and light travel to the Sun's surface and out into the Solar System.

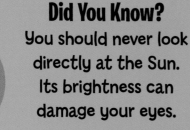

FUN FACTS

Did You Know?
You should never look directly at the Sun. Its brightness can damage your eyes.

Speed of Light
It takes just over eight minutes for light from the Sun to travel all the way to Earth.

Mercury and Venus

Mercury and Venus are the two planets closest to the Sun.
So they are blisteringly hot.

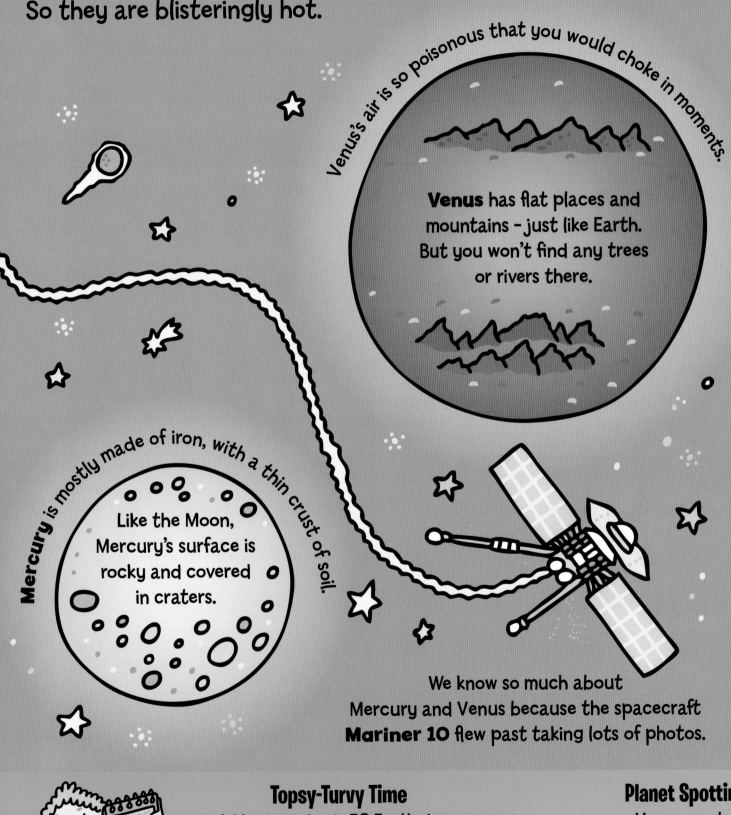

Venus's air is so poisonous that you would choke in moments.

Venus has flat places and mountains – just like Earth. But you won't find any trees or rivers there.

Mercury is mostly made of iron, with a thin crust of soil.

Like the Moon, Mercury's surface is rocky and covered in craters.

We know so much about Mercury and Venus because the spacecraft **Mariner 10** flew past taking lots of photos.

Topsy-Turvy Time
A Mercury day is 58 Earth days.
A year is 88 Earth days.
A Venus year passes in 224 Earth days,
but a day on Venus is 243 Earth days.
How odd!

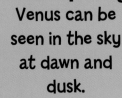

WOW!

Planet Spotting
Venus can be seen in the sky at dawn and dusk.

Mars

Mars is Earth's neighbour. It is sometimes called 'the red planet' because a fine red dust covers its surface.

Winds blow the red dust around, making squiggly dust storms.

Although humans have not yet travelled to Mars, missions are being planned!

Mars is mostly freezing cold and if you drill below the surface you will find huge amounts of ice.

A 'sky crane' would be needed to lower astronauts onto Mars.

Robotic rovers on Mars explore the planet, sending information and pictures back to Earth.

Dried-up rivers show Mars was once a warmer place with water - and maybe life.

Asteroids and Comets

Asteroids are lumps of rock and metal that orbit the Sun.
The belt between Mars and Jupiter contains millions of asteroids.
Some are as big as a house!

Comets orbit the Sun, too.
They are made of ice and dust.
When it's near the Sun, the
comet's melting ice makes a
bright trail in the sky.

Meteors are bits of asteroids
which break off and pass
close to Earth.
As they burn up, it
makes a streak of light
called a shooting star.

Mars

Sometimes meteors crash to Earth,
making a huge, round dip in the
surface, called a crater.

Some people use metal detectors to look
for chunks of meteors, called meteorites.

UPGRADE

Did You Know?
The asteroid Ceres is so big it is now thought of as a dwarf planet.

Halley's Comet
Halley's comet appears once every 75 years.

WOW!

Experts think that a huge meteor crashing to Earth caused the dinosaurs to die out 65 million years ago.

Jupiter

The spacecraft **Dawn** was launched in 2007 to explore the Asteroid belt.

Jupiter

Jupiter is the biggest planet in our Solar System.
Its rocky middle is covered by an ocean of liquid gas,
with poisonous clouds swirling above.

The spacecraft **Juno** is heading to
Jupiter to study how it formed
and what it is made of.

Io

Europa

Jupiter's faint rings were first seen
by the **Voyager 1** and **Voyager 2**
spacecraft.

It is always stormy on Jupiter.
There are hurricane winds and lightning
far more powerful than anything we've seen on Earth.

The spacecraft **Galileo** studied Jupiter and its moons for 14 years.

Ganymede

Jupiter's Great Red Spot is a giant storm that's three times bigger than Earth. It was first seen almost 350 years ago.

Callisto, Io, Europa and Ganymede are four of Jupiter's 60-plus moons.

Callisto

Did You Know?
More than 60 different-sized moons orbit Jupiter. Four of them can be seen at night.

Super-sized Planet
Jupiter is so massive that 1,300 Earths would fit inside it.

WOW!

Jupiter's gravity sucks in lots of comets and asteroids that might otherwise bump into Earth.

Cheers!

Saturn

Saturn is the second largest planet in the Solar System. Like Jupiter, it has a rocky middle covered in liquid with gases swirling above.

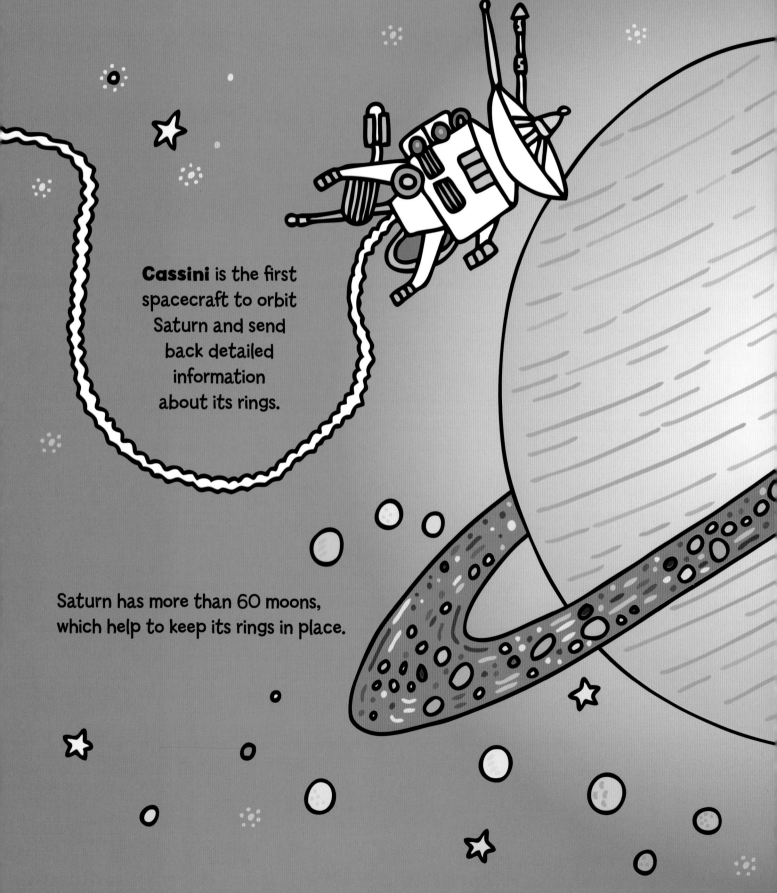

Cassini is the first spacecraft to orbit Saturn and send back detailed information about its rings.

Saturn has more than 60 moons, which help to keep its rings in place.

Saturn has beautiful rings around it, made of ice crystals and rocks, circling the planet at high speed.

The **Huygens** space probe landed on the surface of Titan in 2005. It sent pictures of its surface back to Earth.

Saturn's biggest moon is called **Titan**. It is the only moon known to have its own clouds.

Uranus

No one knows for sure why Uranus spins on its side. Scientists think that long ago something may have crashed into it, tipping it over.

There are 11 rings circling Uranus. They are made of dust, rocks and ice.

Uranus has five large moons and 22 smaller ones that we know of. Some are just several kilometres across.

Did You Know?
Uranus was the first planet to be discovered by a scientist using a telescope.

Big Sleep!
Because it spins on its side, a night on Uranus can last for 40 Earth years!

FUN FACTS

Neptune

Neptune is a similar size to Uranus. But it is a very stormy planet, with some of the strongest winds in all the Solar System.

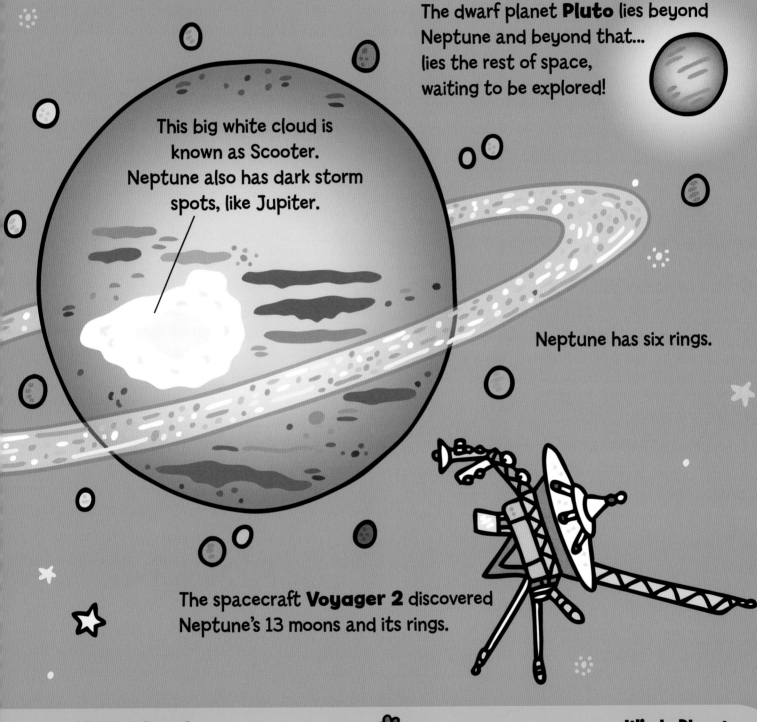

The dwarf planet **Pluto** lies beyond Neptune and beyond that... lies the rest of space, waiting to be explored!

This big white cloud is known as Scooter. Neptune also has dark storm spots, like Jupiter.

Neptune has six rings.

The spacecraft **Voyager 2** discovered Neptune's 13 moons and its rings.

Did You Know?
It took 12 years for **Voyager 2** to reach Neptune.

WOW!

Windy Planet
On Neptune winds blow five times faster than the strongest winds on Earth.

Space Facts

CRIKEY! It would take you around 3,000 years to count all the stars in just one galaxy.

CATCH THAT DRINK!

On the **ISS**, astronauts have to drink from a straw in a sealed container so their drink doesn't float away!

SILENT SPACE

In space, no one can hear you scream... because it is not possible to make a sound when there is no air.

WEIGHTY PROBLEMS

Thanks to gravity, on Mars you would feel much lighter than you do on Earth. On Neptune you'd feel much heavier.

A person celebrating their 10th birthday on Earth has lived for 41 Mercury years and five Martian years!

HAPPY B-EARTH -DAY!